Lift High the Lord

SONGS AND SKETCHES FOR CONTEMPORARY PRAISE
ARRANGED BY JOSEPH LINN

CONTENTS

SKETCHES

Lillenas PUBLISHING COMPANY

KANSAS CITY, MO 64141

Lifted Up Medley

Arr. by Joseph Linn

*"Let My Life Be the Praise" (Dennis and Nan Allen)

life be the praise;_____ be glo - ri - fied__ in all__ __ that I do_____ As a dai-ly re - flec - tion_____ of Your god - ly per - fec - tion._____ Let my

Unison

Unison

Div.

Div.

31 D   D/F♯   G   Bm

35 Em7   D/F♯

A

G   Asus   A   A7

life be the praise,_____ let my life be the praise

to You.

Let my life be the praise_____ to You!_____

50 *"High and Lifted Up" (Debbye Graafsma)

S.A.T. (or S.S.A.) trio

mf

There is no glo - ry in my own wis - dom;

Am7   Bm/D   D7   G   G/B   D/C   C

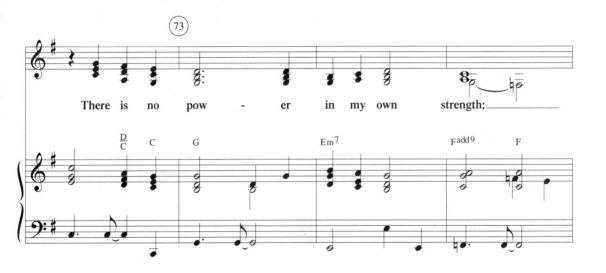

There is no pow - er in my own strength;

D/C   C   G   Em7   Fadd9   F

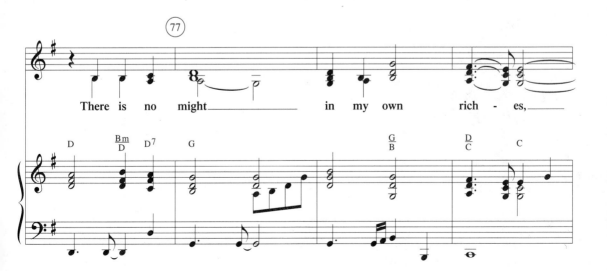

There is no might in my own rich - es,

D   Bm/D   D7   G   G/B   D/C   C

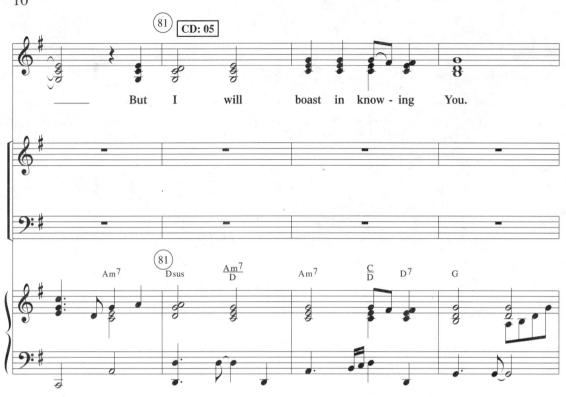

But I will boast in know-ing You.

(Trio) *f*
lift - ed up,____ glo - ry

(Choir)
For You are high and lift - ed up, the glo - ry of the

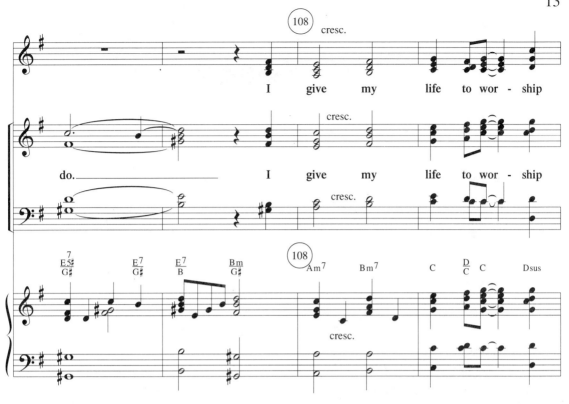

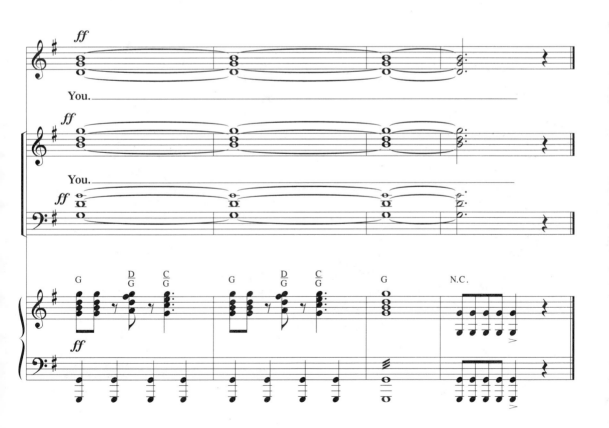

The Stone

Theme: Forgiveness, commitment

Scriptural Background: John 8:1-11; Mark 16:1-2, 9-10

Character: Mary Magdalene—requires an actress capable of solo performance. Careful attention to blocking and movement is necessary to maintain interest and believability.

Setting/Props: This piece works best with very little set or props. The vision of what Mary is saying must be created in the mind of the observer. A costume in keeping with the piece can be used, but current fashion may help the audience "put themselves in her place."

Synopsis: "The Stone" deals specifically with the forgiveness and conversion of Mary Magdalene, but in a broader sense it talks about forgiveness of all sinners and our obligation to share what the Lord has done for us with others who so desperately need Him.

MARY: They were days of endless peril, all of us afraid of our own shadows. We rarely did more than whisper of the days' events, for fear of whose ears might be listening, trying to catch us and carry us away.

I am ashamed to admit that my terror had so overwhelmed me that I actually considered foregoing the trip to the garden with the others. Believe me, I had been sneered at by the mighty Roman guards before, but since they had taken our Lord to His death, things had been changed.

When Jesus was alive it was different. The Romans were afraid of Him. They didn't admit it, but you could see the apprehension in their eyes whenever He came around. They trembled behind their mighty swords when He did nothing more than look their way. After He was gone, they decided to take revenge on His followers, and especially the women. A simple walk down the street became a risk of one's life. And so, many of us, myself included, locked our doors and kept our lamps on a low light, whispering prayers far into the night, hoping that the footsteps outside would pass on down the street, leaving us one more hour of safety.

I made a point of walking with my face down, speaking to no one, hoping to arrive if possible, without incident. Whenever I heard voices approaching I hurried to a doorway, hoping to fade into the background of the dusty street. On the morning of that third day I awoke in a cold sweat, the air was filled with a current of excitement and anxiety. He had spoken to us of this day, many times, but I was in the dark about our future. We were followers of the Son of God, yet too afraid to step out into the light of day. As I prepared my basket of spices I could feel His presence with me, and I wanted to throw my windows open and shout His name into the morning air, but the pounding of my heart rang louder with each breath I took and I finally resolved that today I would stay in. The Lord knew that I loved Him. He would not want me to put myself in danger.

I sat on the bench near the fire and tried to warm the ice away from my aching soul, sorry for myself, sorry for the people who would never know. Then suddenly the room faded before me and I was standing in the streets of the city. The sun was hot on my face, and I could taste the dust in my mouth. My garment was torn and my hair disheveled, and all around me stood an angry, hungry mob. Their eyes burned with the passion of the kill, and in their hands they held my death sentence.

My fear so excited them, they stood for just a moment enjoying their power over me, savoring its intoxicating strength, before they would at last destroy their prey beneath an onslaught of shouts and stones. They were so completely spellbound that they didn't even notice the man pushing His way through the crowd and into the center of the bloodthirsty circle. I saw Him just as He emerged from behind the chief priest, and at the moment of His appearing, my fear dispelled into the mist of His peace. He walked to me as though the others had vanished, their stones turned to dust, their hatred diffused. They shouted to Him to come away from the woman and leave her to her fate or surely He would die with her. Did He even hear them? I couldn't tell. He only bent to help me up from the jaw of my grave and said that I was forgiven. Then He sent me on my way without need for explanation or pleading. As I began to run from the crowd my shame and hatred dropped behind me at the feet of those who sought to kill me. I looked back only once as I ran, but in that instant my heart was bound to His in an unbreakable force. I knew that forever I would belong to Him.

The room cleared, and I was on my face before the fire, weeping over the scene that had just played, aghast at my own lack of courage. Could I deny the one who had pulled me from the darkness of my own sin, the one who risked everything to stand by my side in the midst of savage violence? Would I protect my life out of fear when Someone had given His life for me out of love? I pushed the door open and stepped into the chill of the early moring air. I am coming, Jesus, I could hear myself whispering. I am coming.

Called to Belong to Jesus

L. H.

LARNELLE HARRIS
Arr. by Joseph Linn

Called to walk_____ in His foot - steps,_____

cho - sen____ to bear His name._____

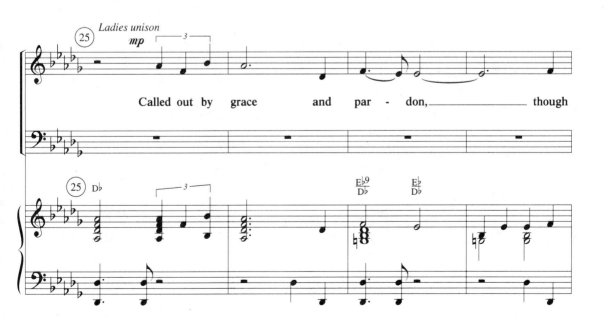

Called out by grace and par - don,_____ though

CD: 07

long to Je - sus.

Absus   Ab   Ab9b

cresc.

Db

44 mf

Called

We are called to be - long   to Je - sus,

mf

44 Dadd9   E9/D   E/D

mf

48

called to a heal - ing place;

48 Gm/E   Gm   D

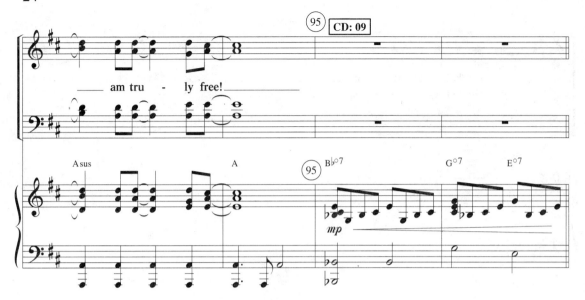

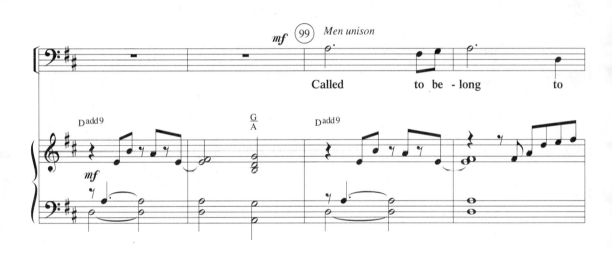

26

What's New?

Theme: Wholeness in Christ

Scriptural Background: 2 Corinthians 5:17

Characters: ONCE BLIND: *a person who was blind but now can see*
(Mark 10:46-52)

ONCE DEAF: *a person who was deaf but now can hear*
(Mark 7:31-37)

ONCE LAME: *a person who was lame but now can walk*
(John 5:1-15)

ONCE CONDEMNED: *a woman who was condemned but
was pardoned* (John 8:1-11)

LEADER: *the worship leader*

Setting/Props: No props are needed. The four characters should be interspersed within the congregation and speak from their respective places. Each character stands to speak until all four are standing in the end.

Synopsis: Four unnamed characters from the Gospels give living testimonies to Christ's power to heal and forgive.

(The worship LEADER steps to the pulpit.)

LEADER: What's new?

ONCE BLIND *(standing):* What's new? My eyes are new. Thanks to Jesus I can see. All my life I lived in total darkness. I saw nothing until the day Jesus touched my eyes. Then in a single moment everything became light. And I can see good. I can see the beauty of this world. And I can also see the ugliness that humanity has created. But, most of all, I can see the face of someone who loves me. I can see Jesus Christ. Are your eyes new?

LEADER: What's new?

ONCE DEAF *(standing):* What's new? My ears are new. Thanks to Jesus I can hear. All my life I lived in a silent world. I heard nothing until the day Jesus touched my ears. Then I heard Him say, "Be opened." And now I can hear birds and music and wonderful noises. I can hear people crying and angry voices. But, most of all, I can hear the words of someone who cares. I can hear Jesus. Are your ears new?

LEADER: What's new?

ONCE LAME *(standing):* What's new? My legs are new. Thanks to Jesus I can run. All my life I was crippled and lame. I crawled from place to place in terrible pain until the day Jesus told me to get up. Then I stood. I walked. I ran. I danced. I can walk in the gardens and run on a mountainside. I can walk through the wilderness and run on a desert. But, most of all, I can walk behind the One who is worth following. I can walk with Jesus. Are your legs new?

LEADER: What's new?

ONCE CONDEMNED *(standing):* What's new? My life is new. Thanks to Jesus I can live. All my life I searched for a reason to live. I was a harlot and a whore until the day I met Jesus. On that day, when I stood condemned, He smiled at me and forgave my every sin. And I found life. Life as it was intended to be. Life full of promise and hope and wonder. Life that, most of all, never ends. In the midst of death, I was pardoned and redeemed by Jesus. I can live in Christ. Is your life new?

ALL *(in unison):* What's new?

LEADER: What's new today in your life? Do you need new eyes? Do you need new ears? Do you need new legs? Do you need a new life? Then come to Jesus Christ who makes all things new (Isaiah 43:18-19).

All I Want Is You, Lord

C. C.

CAROL CYMBALA
Arr. by Joseph Linn

34

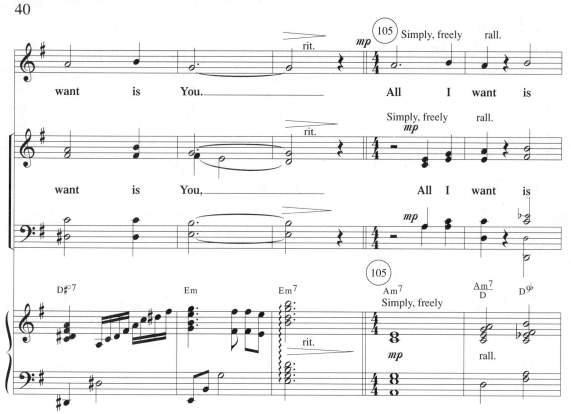

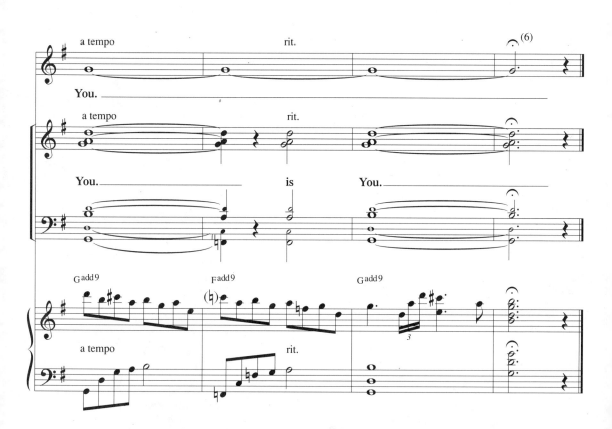

Praise Be to the Name of God Forever

A cappella with percussion

D. W.

DAN WHITTEMORE
Arr. by Joseph Linn

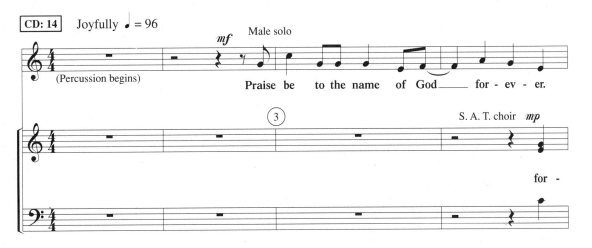

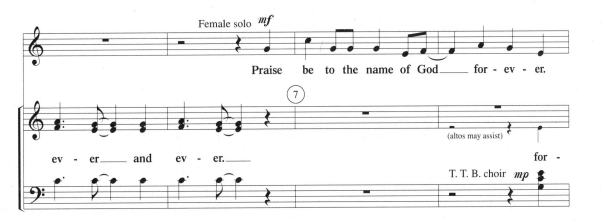

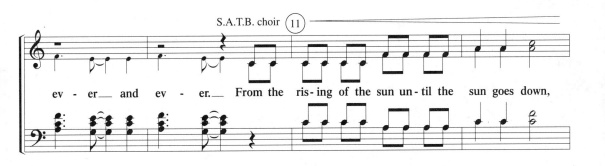

42

43

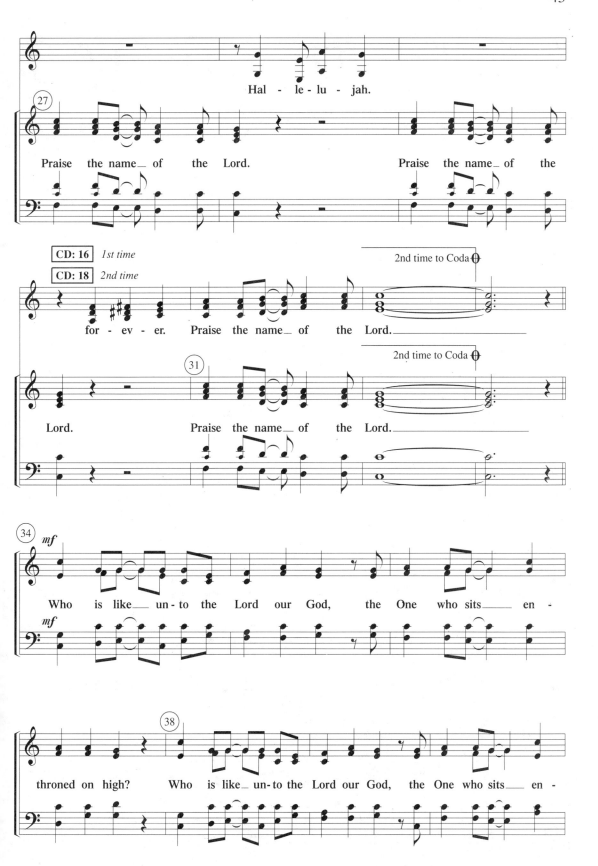

May Your Presence Purify My Heart

KEN BIBLE

STEVEN V. TAYLOR
Arr. by Joseph Linn

52

May Your pres - ence fill my life with praise as my spir - it
wor - ships face to face. Be my beau - ty and the song I raise.
May Your pres - ence fill my life with praise.

The Church Office

Theme: The fruit of faithfulness

Scriptural Background: 1 Corinthians 12:4-31

Characters: JACKIE: *middle-aged, very weary Sunday School superintendent*
DEBBIE: *one of the helpers in the Sunday School office*
BILL: *another helper in the Sunday School office*
JOHN: *a young man who stops by*

Setting/Props: Church office. Basic needs would be a table, a phone, and lots of books, pamphlets, and papers.

Synopsis: We witness a fairly typical Sunday morning in the life of a church Sunday School office, faced with constant chaos and pandemonium. After handling multiple crises and coming to the breaking point, Jackie, the superintendent, rediscovers her purpose for ministry through an unexpected visit by a former student.

(Lights up on the church office. JACKIE *and* DEBBIE *enter.)*

JACKIE *(begins looking through books):* Do you know what they did with the senior high lesson quarterlies?

DEBBIE: I think we're out. Why don't you use the adult quarterlies until they come in?

JACKIE *(thinking):* Might be too advanced. Do you have any junior high?

DEBBIE: Only five. *(Thinking)* But I have seven junior quarterlies.

JACKIE: OK, we'll give them the five junior high, seven junior quarterlies.

DEBBIE: And a box of crayons. The junior lessons all take coloring.

(BILL *enters.)*

BILL *(to* JACKIE): Pick up the telephone. It's Bob.

JACKIE: Don't tell me he's not coming in again. *(Moves to pick up the phone)* What happened—did his cat eat his turtle again? *(Picks up phone)* Hi, Bob. Uh-huh. Yeah. Couldn't you just set the timer? Oh. No. Of course not. I never trust them either. It was just a thought. OK. Thanks for calling. *(Hangs up)* Bob won't be in. Can we get someone else to teach the ninth graders?

DEBBIE: What's wrong with Bob?

JACKIE: He's having relatives over this afternoon and has to put a roast in—so his whole family is staying home.

BILL: It takes a whole family to put a roast in the oven?

JACKIE: I guess so.

DEBBIE: Big roast. *(She grabs a bunch of papers and exits.)*

BILL *(pulling a sheet of paper off of the table):* There must be a mistake here.

JACKIE: What's wrong?

BILL: Eighth grade has six people in class and $250 in offerings.

JACKIE: You better move the decimal point two places to the left.

(DEBBIE enters again.)

DEBBIE: The college class needs some offering envelopes. *(Moves to table, picks up envelopes, looks at them, surprised)*

JACKIE: Again? But I just gave them some.

BILL: The paper airplanes must be flying again.

DEBBIE *(flipping through envelopes):* Do we have any that haven't been drawn on? *(Gasps)* My goodness!

JACKIE: What's wrong?

DEBBIE *(hands envelope to her):* Look.

JACKIE *(looks at envelope, frowns, confused, turns it upside down and looks at it again):* It's either a drawing of the Titanic sinking or Adam and Eve in a car being driven out of the garden of Eden.

BILL *(looking at the envelope):* No, it's a light bulb!

JACKIE *(turning it sideways):* Oops. It's a drawing of the pastor!

DEBBIE: Why is it everyone feels compelled to draw or write all over the pew offering envelopes? *(Exits with envelopes)*

BILL: Because there's no room left on the hymnals.

JACKIE: Remind me to get a chalkboard eraser to the 11th graders.

BILL: Why?

JACKIE: Because their teacher just walked past, and it looks like he's been using his coat sleeve again.

(DEBBIE *enters.*)

DEBBIE: Alfred is on the phone. *(Exits)*

JACKIE *(picks up the phone):* Hello? Yes. Uh-huh. Stubbed your toe? I'll bet it is painful. Sure. Sailing? I don't really know if it is good therapy for toe problems. Well . . . if you think so . . . Bye. *(Hangs up)*

BILL: Sailing for a stubbed toe? That's a new one. *(Grabs some papers and exits)*

JACKIE: Now we need a fourth grade teacher.

(DEBBIE *enters.*)

DEBBIE: Where's a mop?

JACKIE: Why? What's wrong?

DEBBIE: Alan got sick in class.

JACKIE: Eating glue again?

DEBBIE: Crayons this time. Red, white, and blue. *(Exits)*

JACKIE: Very patriotic. *(Begins flipping through papers. Bill enters.)*

BILL: You better pick up the phone.

JACKIE: What now?

BILL: It's the manager at the 7-11 *(or equivalent convenience store)*—he says a bunch of our teenagers are down there.

JACKIE: Who?

BILL: Same as last time.

JACKIE: I thought we assigned someone to stay by the door and make sure the kids don't sneak off?

BILL: We did. Bob. *(Exits)*

JACKIE: Oh. And he's home with the family loading a roast in the oven. I should have told him to rent a forklift. *(Picks up phone)* Hello? Yes? I'll have someone come down to get them in a minute. No, they are not supposed to be there. No, it's not really a church-sponsored prayer breakfast. How many candy bars? Tell them they have to pay for them themselves. Thank you. *(Hangs up)* They told the manager they were having a prayer breakfast and wanted to charge a bunch of candy bars to our account.

(DEBBIE *enters.*)

DEBBIE: They're out of diapers in the nursery.

JACKIE: Oh no. Is there anything we can use?

DEBBIE: How about some old lesson quarterlies?

JACKIE *(shakes head):* No. Leaves printer's ink. The parents'll get suspicious.

DEBBIE: They didn't notice last time.

JACKIE: A few of them did. They thought we had tattooed drawings of David and Goliath on their children's bottoms. Oh, can you do me a favor while you're at the store?

DEBBIE: I didn't know I was going.

JACKIE: A few of our kids are there.

DEBBIE: Again? Couldn't we just leave them this time?

JACKIE: I would, but the manager knows who we are.

(DEBBIE *exits.* BILL *enters.)*

BILL: Have you seen Gloria?

JACKIE: Why?

BILL: They need some entertainment in the 12th grade class. Real quick. I thought she could do some chalk talks or something.

JACKIE: In the 12th grade class?

BILL: They're bored. They're starting to get restless.

JACKIE: Where's Steve? He's supposed to be teaching them!

BILL: He was until the chalkboard fell on him.

JACKIE: It did? But it's nailed to the wall.

BILL: I guess the chair knocked it off.

JACKIE: Chair? How could a chair—?

BILL: It was thrown against it.

JACKIE: Thrown! Why would . . . ?

BILL: When the fire started, people panicked.

JACKIE: Fire! What fire?

BILL: The one that started when the ceiling fell in.

JACKIE: How did the ceiling fall in?

BILL: Rick Daniels pulled it down with him.

JACKIE: Rick? What was Rick Daniels doing up there?

BILL: They threw him up and he had to come down sometime.

JACKIE: Why did they do that?

BILL: Because he threw his Bible at Brian.

JACKIE: Why did he throw his Bible at Brian.

BILL: Because Brian wrote on him with a pen.

JACKIE: Forget it! Forget it! That's it! I quit! This is supposed to be Sunday School—not a zoo! We're supposed to be teaching kids the Bible, helping to mold and shape their lives for God, but instead it's one gigantic kindergarten! All we do is coddle them—baby-sit them! What's the point? Why are we doing this? I can't take it anymore! I'm through!

(JOHN enters—looks around sheepishly.)

JOHN: Hello?

(This stops JACKIE from her tirade. She and BILL look at JOHN.)

BILL: Can we help you?

JOHN: Yes. My name's John Wilson.

JACKIE: John Wilson? Not the John Wilson that I taught back in . . . (Gestures with her hand held low) Why, you must have been this high.

JOHN: That's me.

JACKIE: I haven't seen you in years. What's happening?

JOHN: That's why I'm here. I wanted to stop in and let you know that because of the love and patience you showed me in that class, I've accepted a call to the ministry. At a time when everyone else kept giving up on me, you stayed in there. I want to thank you for that.

JACKIE (speechless): That's wonderful, John.

JOHN: Well, that's about it. I was in town visiting my folks . . . Well, God bless you, and thanks. (He exits. JACKIE and BILL look at each other—not knowing what to make of it.)

BILL: As you were saying . . . ?

JACKIE (begins digging into the pile of papers again): Have you seen the sixth grade roll book?

BILL (begins looking with her): It was here a minute ago . . . (They begin searching through the papers. The lights fade.)

Blackout

Heaven Is Counting on You

R. B. and S. M.

RAY BOLTZ and STEVE MILLIKAN
Arr. by Joseph Linn

CD: 25

Heav - en__ is count - ing__ on you._____ We are

Unison   *Div.*   *Unison*

D add 9   A sus   G no 3rd add 9

stand - ing_____ at the end of__ time;__ we are

D   D sus   D

part of__ a grand de - sign. We are grate - ful__ to a

D   B m   C no 3rd add 9   D

63

66

CD: 29

cheer us on to - day.

Heav - en is count - ing on you; run with a heart that is

true. Car - ry the cross, reach - ing the lost.

His Power Medley

Arr. by Joseph Linn

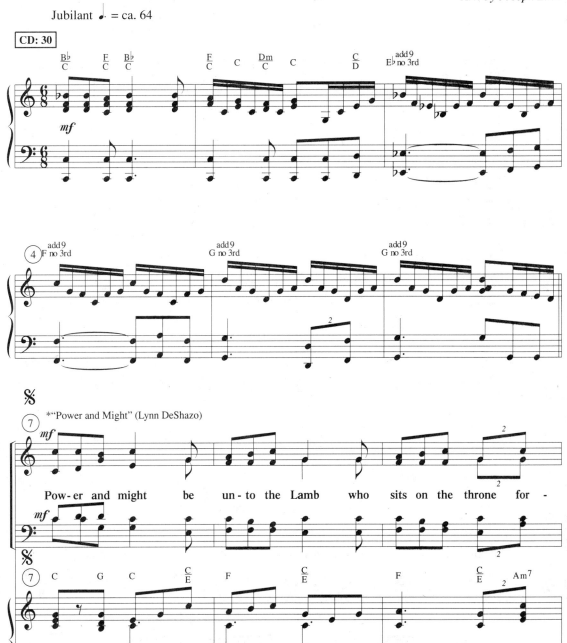

ev - er. Glo - ry and light il - lu - mine His own, who

wor - ship the Lamb for - ev - er - more.

People from ev - 'ry na - tion and tribe will praise the great I

Lord God at all_ times. I will sing His praise the rest of my years.

I sought the Lord_ and He gra-cious-ly an-swered. He took a-way_ from me

Unison

my great-est fear. He took a-way_ from me my great-est

73

strong arm sur-rounds__ me. By grace He has saved me and

I'll nev-er die.

I will lift high_____ the Lord God at all__ times. I will sing His praise the

The Lamb Has Overcome

C. C.

CAROL CYMBALA
Arr. by Joseph Linn

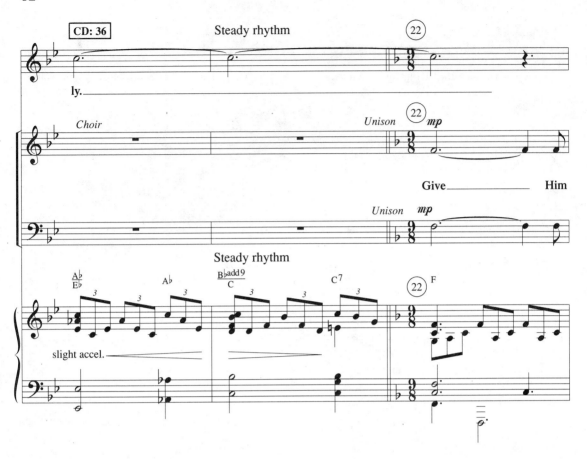

CD: 37

wor - thy;_____ the Lamb has o - ver - come._____

Give Him glo - ry,_____
Give_____ Him glo - ry,_____

praise and hon - or._____ He is
praise_____ and hon - or._____ Je - sus_____ is

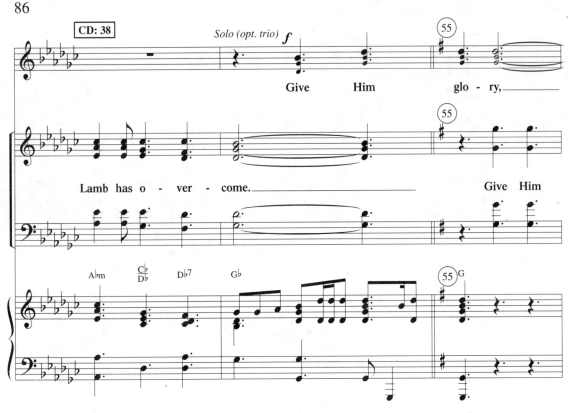

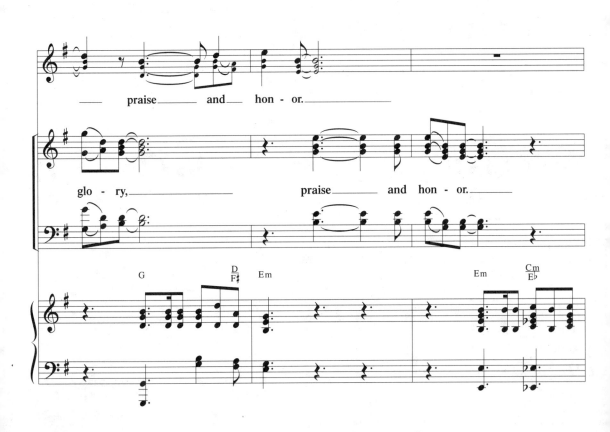

88

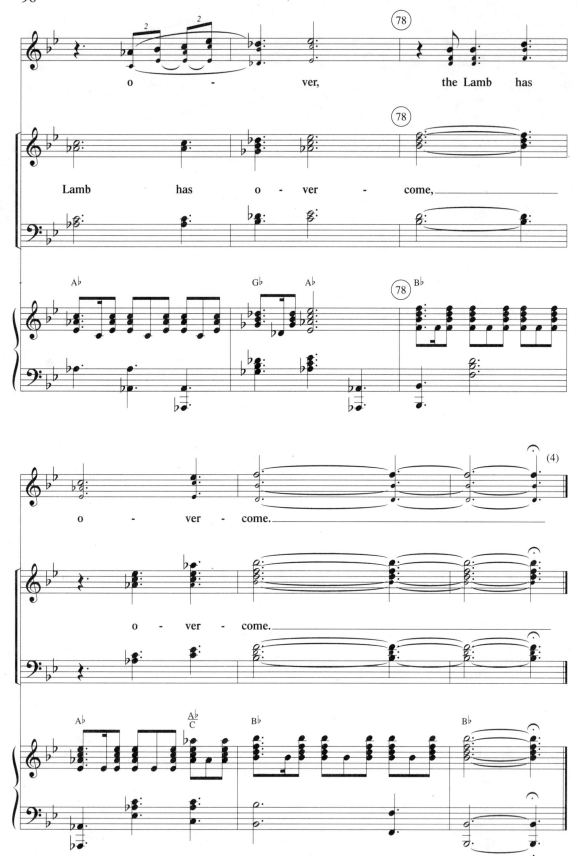

Round and Round

Theme: Aging, sickness, does God exist or care?

Scriptural Background: Matthew 6:25-34; Isaiah 55:6-9

Characters: STEVE: *a 38-year-old father*
JOY: *his 33-year-old wife*
MEGAN: *their seven-year-old daughter*

Setting/Props: A living room

Synopsis: Steve, a 38-year-old father, has just returned from visiting his father in a nursing home. His father is ill with Alzheimer's disease. His wife, Joy, and their daughter enter, returning from a final dress rehearsal for the daughter's ballet recital. Steve's spirits are temporarily lifted by his daughter's excitement and enthusiasm, but after she leaves, he reveals his deep pain and frustration to his wife regarding his father's degenerating condition. He is also afraid that in 30 years, his daughter will witness him in the same condition. In a touching conclusion, the daughter returns and tries to comfort her dad. Steve questions how a "god" could allow such things as Alzheimer's but is surprised by his daughter's response.

(*As the scene opens,* STEVE *is fumbling aimlessly through the paper. He throws it down, frustrated and discouraged. He closes his eyes and tries to fall asleep.* JOY *enters with* MEGAN. *They are singing.* MEGAN *is wearing a dance recital outfit. At first they do not see* STEVE.)

JOY (*as she swings* MEGAN): You do the Hokey Pokey and you turn yourself around. That's what it's all about. So what do you think? Can I be in the recital with you?

MEGAN: Mom, that's not exactly ballet.

JOY: You don't think so?

MEGAN: That's kind of baby stuff.

JOY: So I guess you'll have to be a star by yourself.

MEGAN: I hope I won't be too nervous in front of all those people.

JOY: Are you kidding? You'll be fabulous! (JOY *sees* STEVE *sleeping. She motions to* MEGAN *to be quiet, then sneaks up behind* STEVE *and makes the sound of a trumpet fanfare.* STEVE *jumps.*) Ladies and gentlemen, especially daddies, may I introduce to you the one, the only, the amazing Megan Renae. (*Cheers and claps.* STEVE *joins in whistling and* MEGAN *curtsies.*) You should've seen her at rehearsal. She was great! She really wowed 'em.

MEGAN: Oh, Dad, I wasn't that good. But I did it all right, every step.

JOY: No, she wasn't good, she was fabulous! Made me want to put on a pair of tights and join the show.

STEVE (*really starts clapping and cheering*): Now that would be worth seeing!

(JOY *coughs disapprovingly.*)

STEVE: I mean, seeing my little girl!

MEGAN (*climbing on* STEVE's *lap*): Daddy, you're coming tomorrow night to see me, aren't you?

STEVE: Of course. Wouldn't miss it. Will it be as long as last year? (JOY *shoots him a less than approving look and coughs.*) I mean, I wish you were doing the whole show.

MEGAN: I would get too tired. You should see the baby dancers. They're very funny.

JOY: And they're very cute!

(JOY *does a little Hokey Pokey and* MEGAN *laughs.*)

MEGAN: Don't worry, Dad, I'm better than that.

JOY (*pretends to be hurt*): Hey! (*Laughs, taking* MEGAN's *hand and leading her away*) Now, my lovely dancing bear, you need to take off that costume before it gets dirty, ripped, or anything worse.

MEGAN: Please, can't I wear it a little longer?

JOY: No. You were not blessed with a mother who can put things back together. If something happens to that costume, you'll have to dance in your pajamas.

MEGAN (*pleading*): Mom! I'd be careful.

JOY: Show time will come soon enough. Now scoot!

MEGAN: Daddy wants to see my dance first, right, Dad? (STEVE *isn't listening.*) Right, Dad?

STEVE: What?

JOY: Megan, go!

MEGAN: Dad?

STEVE *(his mind is elsewhere):* Obey your mother.

MEGAN: But you're coming tomorrow night?

STEVE *(with a touch of gruffness):* I said I was.

JOY: Daddy and I need to talk now. Get changed. That's an order. (MEGAN *leaves; to* STEVE) Are you OK?

STEVE: Sure. So she's really good, huh?

JOY: Well, she's not exactly ready to dance with the New York City Ballet, but she's coming along. Oh, Steve, watching Megan brought back so many memories. Did you know I took lessons for a couple of years? I was kind of Queen Klutz, but I tried. Luckily Megan doesn't take after me. I remember my first recital. (JOY *notices that* STEVE *is trying to act interested but is very distracted.)* What's wrong, Steve?

STEVE: Nothing really, I'm just tired.

JOY: It's more than that. My silly memories are the last thing on your mind right now. What's going on?

STEVE: I went to see my dad at the nursing home this afternoon.

JOY: Is he worse?

STEVE: Physically, he's about the same, but mentally . . . he asked me three times if I remembered to put the trash out for my mother. Then after I'd been there a half hour, he asked when I came and why didn't someone tell him I was there.

JOY: I'm sorry, Steve.

STEVE: The nurses said he spits food at them sometimes now. And, Joy, he swore a blue streak at one of the other residents for blocking his view of the TV with his wheelchair. My dad never swore! He's not the same man anymore.

JOY: You should have waited until I got home. I would have gone with you.

STEVE: He's my father, for heaven's sake! It sickens me to see him. There's something wrong with this picture!

JOY: It's Alzheimer's, Steve. It's not him.

STEVE: He taught me to ride a bike and how to play ball. (STEVE *remembers sadly.)* He never missed a ball game. I used to point him out to all the other kids 'cause he was so strong. He could hit a ball into the neighbor's pasture! Now he can't even control his own body functions.

JOY: I know it must be hard.

STEVE: Round and round . . . is that all there is?

JOY: What?

STEVE: Will you be left to try to make sense of it all like my mom? Will Megan end up trying to tell me about her daughter's recital or her son's ball game while I babble into space about taking out the garbage?

JOY: I don't know. Only God does, I guess.

STEVE: God? (*Picks up the paper*) Why would any God let the world get so crazy? (*Tosses the paper*) Is aging and disease His sick joke on humanity? I mean, if He exists, can't He see what's happening to my dad? Can't He hear and feel Dad's pain, my pain . . . (*there is a long pause as they both try to comprehend* STEVE's *last words;* MEGAN *enters behind her parents and looks puzzled;* STEVE *repeats softly*) . . . round and round.

MEGAN: What, Daddy? Do you want to see me go round and round? (MEGAN *dances excitedly.*)

JOY (*startled*): Megan, I told you to take off your outfit.

MEGAN: I can't undo the snaps myself.

JOY: I'm sorry. Come here. I didn't mean to be so gruff.

(STEVE *is still looking off sadly in the opposite direction.*)

MEGAN: What's the matter with Daddy?

JOY: He's just a little sad right now, Honey.

MEGAN: Why are you sad, Daddy? (*She tugs on his arm.*) Daddy?

(STEVE *picks her up and almost cries as he holds her close.*)

STEVE: Daddy is sad because he went to see his daddy today.

MEGAN: You have a daddy?

JOY: Grandpa's his daddy. Grandpa was once a young man with children, and Daddy was his little boy.

MEGAN: For real, Daddy?

(STEVE *nods.*)

STEVE (*quietly*): Grandpa's very sick.

JOY: But he was once tall and strong and handsome just like our daddy.

MEGAN: Why'd he change?

STEVE: I don't know, Princess. *(Very difficult for* STEVE *to explain)* He got a little older and then he suddenly started to get sick.

MEGAN: He's got Old Timer's disease, right?

STEVE *(faint but sad smile):* Alzheimer's, yes. No one knows why some people get it.

MEGAN: Just God knows.

(STEVE *sets her down and comes down to her level.)*

STEVE: Do you think there's a God, Megan?

MEGAN: Of course, Daddy. 'Cause there's music and ballet and ice cream. Somebody had to think of that good stuff. (MEGAN *hugs* STEVE.) I love you, Daddy. Can I show Laura my dance?

JOY: One time! Then you get back here and I'll help you get off that costume.

(MEGAN *runs off.* JOY *puts her arms around* STEVE.)

JOY: Did you hear her? I love you, too, Daddy.

STEVE: Ballet, ice cream, . . . all that good stuff. If only it could be that simple.

JOY: Maybe it is . . . maybe it is.

I Go to Jesus

D. W.

DAN WHITTEMORE
Arr. by Joseph Linn

In tempo, with a shuffle feel

When I need a friend I can de-pend on,

I go to Je-sus. He is my

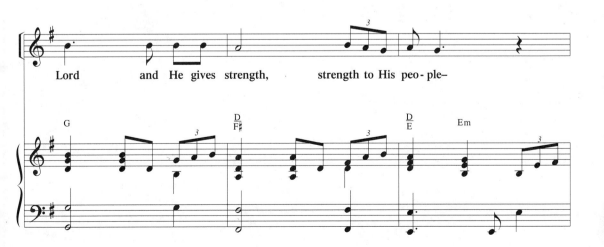

Lord and He gives strength, strength to His peo-ple–

26

Al - might - y God, and He bless - es them with His peace.

C/D Gsus/D G B A/C♯ B7/D♯ Em Em add9

30

When I need strength, hope, or a friend,

A♯°7 C♯°7 E°7 Bm CM7 G/B B♭°7 Am9 Am7

34

I go to Je - sus.

Am/D C/D G D/F♯ D/E Em

38 CD: 40

D/F♯ G D/F♯ D/E Em

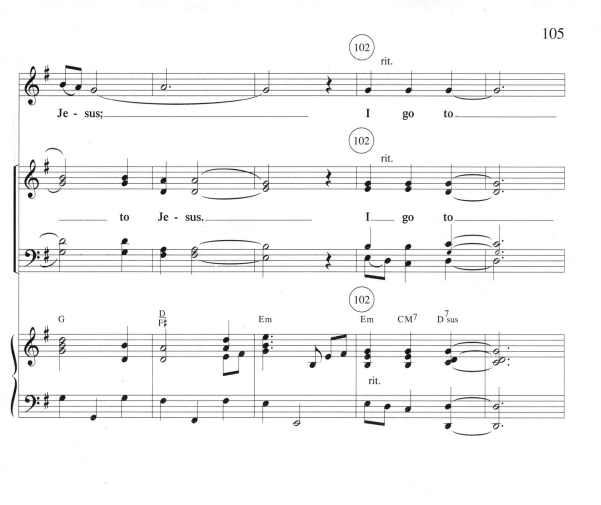

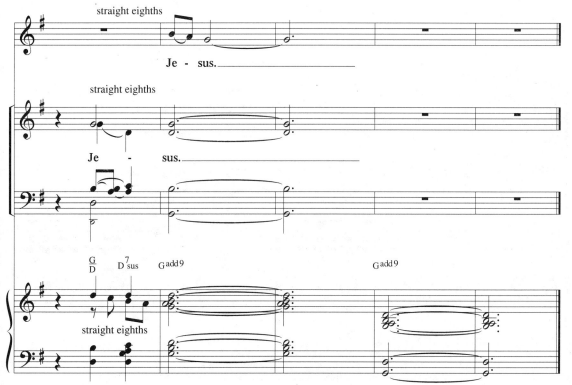

Hosanna to the King

D. D.

DANNY DAVIS and JOSEPH LINN
Arr. by Joseph Linn

CD: 43

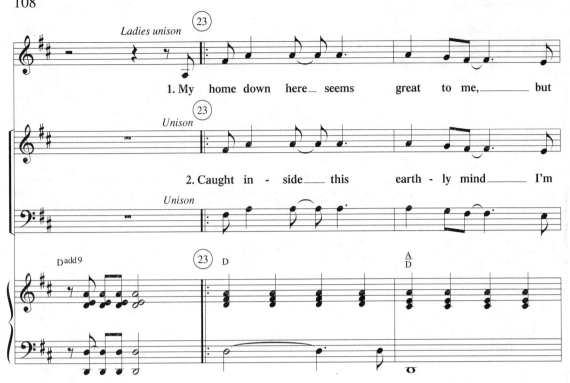

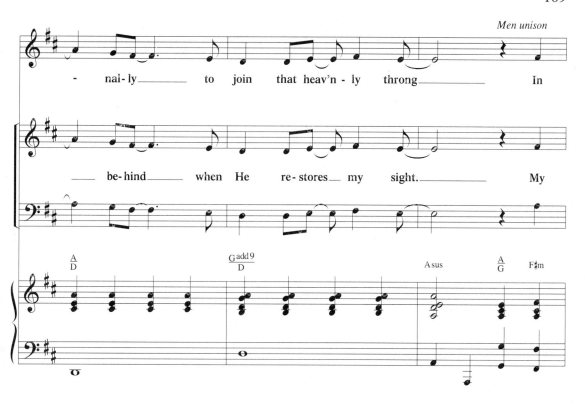

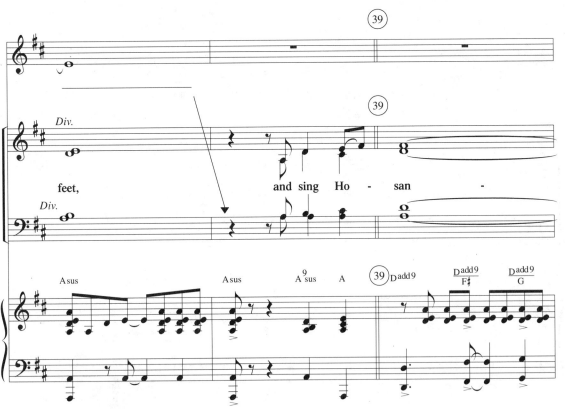

112

*"When the Roll Is Called Up Yonder"
(James M. Black)

And the glo - ries of His res - ur - rec - tion share,

When the saved of earth____ shall gath - er to their

home be - yond the skies–____ When the roll is called_ up

God's Busy?

Theme: Taking time to talk to God

Scriptural Background: Psalm 139:17-18; Isaiah 65:24

Characters: JEFF: *average guy, guilty of neglecting time with God*
ANGEL: *voice offstage, a receptionist*
EDNA: *voice offstage, public relations for God*

Setting/Props: No set or props are required. Muzak is needed. It is suggested that offstage voices be amplified.

Synopsis: Jeff attempts to explain to God why he's been unable to spend time with Him, only to be put on hold by a heavenly receptionist. After Jeff gets a taste of the same neglect he's shown his Maker, he understands how God must feel. Edna, a PR person, puts Jeff right on through to God.

(JEFF *is center stage holding an imaginary conversation with God.*)

JEFF: God, hi, um . . . it's me, Jeff Spaulding. Boy, it's been a while, hasn't it? You can't imagine how swamped I've been. Actually, I guess You can. So, You know what it's been like and You understand that I really had to take that extra project at work. The boss really appreciated my initiative, and that extra money will really help pull down my Visa bill. Now, I know You're thinking that I could have given up that hour or so I spent at the gym every day, but my body's a temple, like You say, and I have to stay in shape for church softball. Those Thursday night practices are a great excuse for good Christian fellowship and trips to Dairy Queen—as are those Saturday night games. Now, Saturday is for the kids, Tuesday is TV night, and Wednesday's for Debbie. I do have every intention of joining one of those Monday night Bible studies just as soon as football season ends. In the event of a football players' strike, I promise You I'll join earlier. All right, here's the good news: I'm going to start reading the Bible just as soon as I finish the last half of *War and Peace*—

ANGEL (*interrupting, an offstage voice*): Will you hold please?

JEFF: Sure . . . What?!

(Muzak is heard for a moment, then goes off.)

ANGEL: Name please.

JEFF: Jeff Spaulding. Excuse me, who—?

ANGEL: Jeff, God's very busy today. Could He get back to you tomorrow?

JEFF: Sure . . . no . . . wait a second. I'll be out of the office tomorrow. Hey, who—?

ANGEL: Jeff, in that case you'll have to fax us your prayer. We'll file it and get back to you in six to eight weeks.

JEFF: But I can't wait that long!

ANGEL: Do you wish to file a complaint?

JEFF: I guess so . . .

ANGEL: Please hold.

(Muzak is heard again for a moment.)

EDNA *(an offstage voice):* Yes?

JEFF *(shocked by a woman's voice):* God?

EDNA: No, I'm Edna—public relations. What may I do for you?

JEFF: I'm trying to talk to God. Isn't He in?

EDNA *(laughs):* Of course He's in. What do you think, He's out golfing?

JEFF: Forgive me, but I was under the impression—

EDNA *(interrupting):* Hey, listen, buddy, God's swamped. There's this Middle East thing,* hunger, poverty, souls falling to the left and right . . .

JEFF: Yeah, I know, but I had a really bad day.

EDNA *(patronizing):* Ahh!

JEFF: Don't patronize me!

EDNA: Hey, Gabriel, get this! Jeff had a bad day!

JEFF: Stop that!

EDNA: We're crying a river for you up here, Jeff.

JEFF: Please! I need help down here.

---

*Or another current "hot" topic.

EDNA: Jeff, according to our records, we haven't heard from you in quite awhile.

JEFF: I know. I've been busy.

EDNA: Too busy to talk to your Maker?

JEFF: All right! I know it. I've given Him no time. I'm sorry, OK. I'm sorry. Just send God a memo that says, "Jeff Spaulding's sorry."

EDNA *(beat, then):* Jeff?

JEFF: What?

EDNA: I'll put you right through.

(JEFF *smiles as lights fade.*)

He Never Sleeps

TRADITIONAL

TRADITIONAL
Arr. by Joseph Linn

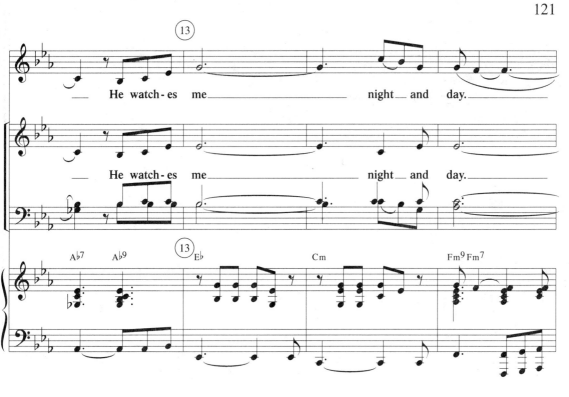

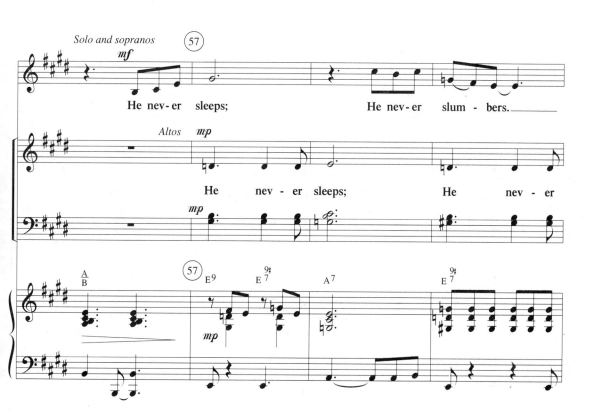

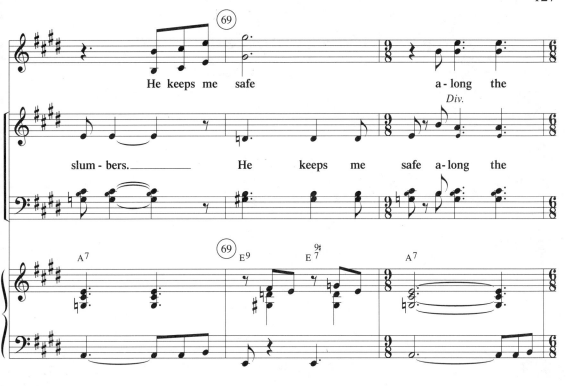

He keeps me safe a - long the

slum - bers._____ He keeps me safe a - long the

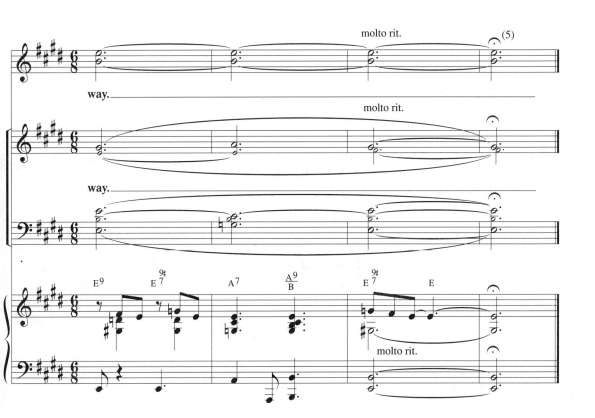

way.

way.

Mercy Instead

MELODY LINN

JOSEPH and MELODY LINN
Arr. by Joseph Linn

is the least that I can give_____ To a fi-cient_____ to____ cov - er all_____ my sin; When my

Ah

CD: 52 *1st time*
CD: 54 *2nd time*

God who came to earth_____ and died so I could____ live.

heart is____ un - faith-ful, Your mer - cy be - gins.

Your____ mer - cy be - gins.

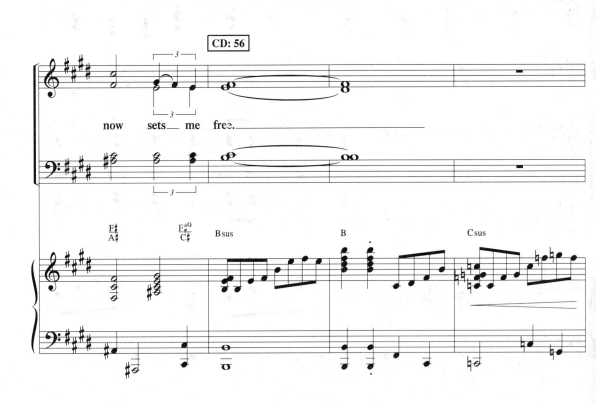

He sac-ri-ficed all; I sac-ri-ficed

He sac-ri-ficed all;

Csus   F   Bb

some. I need-ed a Sav-ior;

I sac-ri-ficed some. Ah

F   Bb/C   F   F

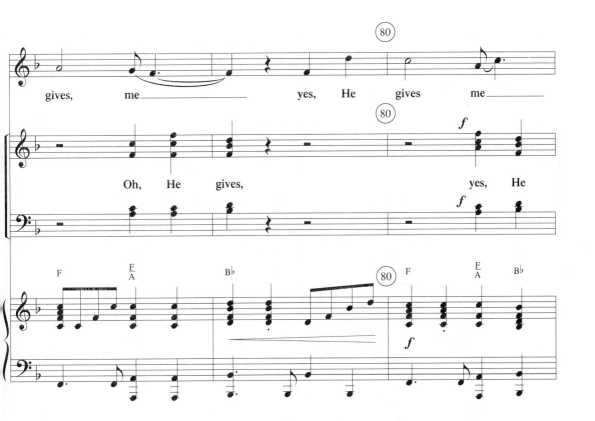

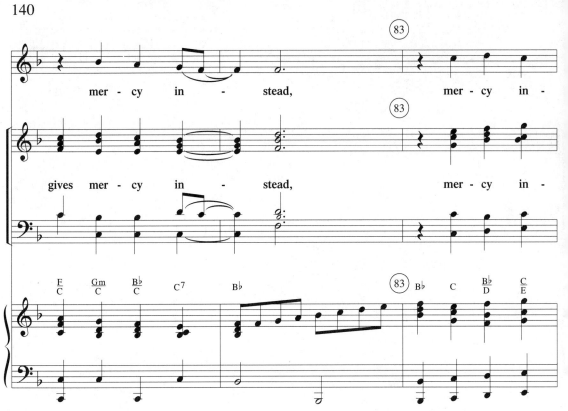

mer - cy in - stead,   mer - cy in -

gives mer - cy in - stead,   mer - cy in -

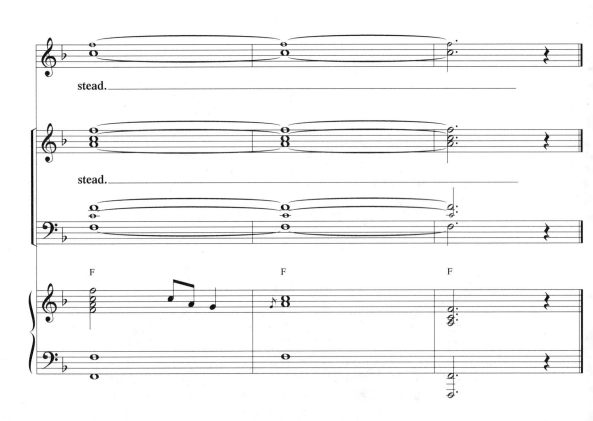

stead.

stead.